For Mark and Kelsey, my energized nephew and niece, with love!

Chariot Victor Publishing
Cook Communications, Colorado Springs, CO 80918
Cook Communications, Paris, Ontario
Kingsway Communications, Eastbourne, England

DESERTS AND JUNGLES
© 1999 by Michael Carroll

ISBN 0-78143-275-8
Designed by Thomason Design Center
First printing, 1999
Printed in Singapore
03 02 01 00 99   5 4 3 2 1

Paintings by Michael Carroll

Photo Credits:
p. 3 Joshua tree in the California desert (Michael Carroll)
p. 5, p. 7 Tropical rain forests of Hawaii (Michael Carroll)
p. 5, p. 7 Desert of Death Valley (Michael Carroll)
p. 5, p. 30 Jungle (David Craig)
p. 5, p. 13 Bryce Canyon (Michael Carroll)
p. 5, p. 24 Redwood trees (Michael Carroll)
p. 5, p. 12, p. 30 Monument Valley (Michael Carroll)
p. 9 Hot deserts of Utah (Michael Carroll)
p. 10 Desert cactus (Michael Carroll)
p. 12 Arches National Monument (Michael Carroll)
p. 14 Antarctica (Dale Andersen)
p. 14 Mauna Kea, Hawaii (Michael Carroll)
p. 17 Qumran (Duane Cory)
p. 18 Deserts of Palestine (Duane Cory)
p. 19 Fortress in the Judean wilderness (Duane Cory)
p. 20 A dense forest (Michael Carroll)
p. 22 Brightly colored birds (Bill Gerrish)
p. 23 Iguassu Falls (David Craig)
p. 25 Zion National Park (Bill Gerrish)
p. 25 Yosemite National Park (Michael Carroll)
p. 26 Boreal forests (Michael Carroll)
p. 26 Neuschawanstein Castle (Michael Carroll)
p. 29 Farmers clear the land (Duane Cory)
p. 30 Lichens (Michael Carroll)
p. 31 Rain forest (Michael Carroll)
p. 31 Salt lake beds (Michael Carroll)
p. 31 Sand dunes (Michael Carroll)

DESERTS AND JUNGLES

Michael Carroll

Chariot Victor Publishing
A Division of Cook Communications

DESERTS AND JUNGLES

…Since the creation of the world God's…power and divine nature…have been clearly seen…from what has been made.
Romans 1:20

Ever since God spoke the universe into being, our Earth has been changed and shaped by many powerful things. The wind roars and the rain falls. Weather makes some places wet and others dry.

Jungles grow where it is very wet. They are rich in fruits, vegetables, and wood. Forests and jungles are the homes of many of God's creatures. The wild and wacky animals and insects that live there make all kinds of noise, especially at night when many wake up. The jungle is a lively place.

Other places on our world get almost no rain at all. Some are cold and some are hot, but all are very dry. These places are called *deserts*. Deserts are just as wonderful as jungles, but in different ways.

Above **The tropical rain forests of Hawaii and the deserts of Death Valley show us the wonderful contrasts in God's world.**

The desert is a quiet place. Often, the only sound you can hear is a faint breeze or a bug chirping. But deserts are exciting, too. Much of the excitement is under the sand, where creatures spend hot days trying to keep cool. At night, the snakes, owls, tarantulas, and other creatures come out to explore and hunt for food.

Plants in these places are quite different, too. Jungles have plants with leaves. In the dry desert, cacti grow spines with which to collect water.

Deserts and jungles are not alike, but God loves them both. Jungles were created for special reasons, and so were deserts. Let's see what each place is like.

Left **Deserts and jungles are very different places.**

DESERTS—GOD'S NATURE SHOW

He turned rivers into a desert, flowing springs into thirsty ground.
Psalm 107:33

We think of deserts as places full of hot, dry sand. But if you go to a desert, bring more than your sunglasses. You might need an umbrella or even a coat! Deserts can be hot during the day and cold at night. And even though all deserts are dry, sometimes thunderstorms come that create floods.

There are two kinds of deserts—hot and cold. The little water that comes to hot deserts falls as rain, while cold deserts get their water from snow.

Deserts have been called "God's Nature Show." There are few plants or trees to hide the earth, so it is easy to see how God put the world together. You can see mountains of bare rock, drifting sand dunes, and swirling mini-tornadoes called *dust devils.* You can also see *mesas,* stone arches, and bright white *salt lake beds.* The rocks and sand make beautiful shapes. In the desert, you can watch the wind, rain, and sun shaping the mountains and rocks around you.

The Bible mentions deserts often, especially in the Psalms. Moses, Abraham, Isaac, and many other Bible people made their homes in the desert. But the Bible lands have just a few of the deserts in the world. Deserts are found in many places, on every continent on Earth.

Right **This mountain of bare rock is in the hot deserts of Utah.**
Left **Delicate flowers bloom in even the driest deserts.**
Above Left **The world map shows us the desert areas.**

DESERT LIFE

The wild animals honor me, the jackals and the owls, because I provide water in the desert and streams in the wasteland, to give drink to my people, my chosen.　　Isaiah 43:20

Deserts are not all sand and rock. Forests of cacti, bright fields of flowers, colorful lizards and birds, and exotic creatures such as camels and scorpions live there.

Plants and animals of the desert are protected from their enemies and the elements in many clever ways. The most important thing they need to do is to get water. The cactus does this by growing needles which make shade, collect dew each night, and keep them from getting eaten. Needles keep the air calm near the cactus so its skin doesn't dry out. Cactus roots stay near the surface to soak up any rain that comes along. When it rains, cacti swell up and store water for the dry times. A giant *Saguaro* cactus can grow as high as eight adults standing on each other's shoulders, and it can hold six tons of water inside!

Desert creatures don't have wide roots to catch water or thorns to keep cool, but they do have tricks to keep them alive and happy. During the day, lizards and snakes stay in the shade under rocks or bury themselves in sand. They come out only at night. Some birds fly to *oases* or lakes to drink and cool off. When they return to the nest, their chicks drink the water in their feathers! Other creatures get water from the things they eat—seeds, plants, and other animals. Some, like the oryx, kangaroo rats, and cockroaches, can go their entire lives without a drink.

Tarantulas are poisonous desert creatures. These hairy spiders are the size of your hand. Their bite hurts, but is not serious to humans. Scorpion and rattlesnake bites can send you to the hospital, so stay away!

Above Flowers and thorns grow together on this beautiful desert cactus.
Right The world's deserts are full of many living things.

The Deserts of the Southwest

I will put in the desert the cedar and the acacia, the myrtle and the olive. I will set pines in the wasteland, the fir and the cypress together. Isaiah 41:19

Some of the most beautiful deserts in the world are in the southwestern United States. Arches National Monument in Utah is named for the natural arches that form in its pink sandstone. The longest arch, called Landscape Arch, is as long as twenty-seven cars! The rocks in this park form strange and wonderful shapes, and have names like the "Three Sisters," the "Parade of Elephants," and even "Duck on the Rock." Nearby is another desert area called Goblin Valley, where the rocks look like enormous mushrooms. Utah's Bryce Canyon is a high desert known for its strange canyon walls.

Above **The colorful walls of Bryce canyon are worn into weird shapes.**

Beyond these places is a huge area called Monument Valley. This area has mesas—rocky tops sticking out of piles of sand and gravel. Monument Valley is a very special place to the Navajo people, who have lived in the valley for 400 years.

Another famous desert is Death Valley in California. The lowest place in North America is here in a salty lake called Badwater (sound yummy?). Death Valley gets as hot as 120°F. Like many deserts, it has ponds or lakes that come and go. Brine shrimp lay eggs that can dry out and still be fresh for twenty-five years. When the rain comes again, the eggs hatch. Some toads spend nine months out of each year in a burrow underground. When raindrops come, they wake up again, eat bugs, lay eggs, and get ready for the next time they have to "dig in."

Left **Monument Valley is a desert in the southwestern United States that has flat-topped rocks called mesas.**
Left Inset **A stone arch carved by wind and water, in Arches National Monument.**

COLD DESERTS

…But there was no water for the people to drink.
Exodus 17:1

There are some deserts that are never hot, but they are still very dry. Cold deserts can be found in Antarctica, Canada, Russia, Greenland, and Iceland. These places get very little *precipitation* (rain or snow), and what water they have is almost always frozen. Africa's hot Sahara Desert, the biggest desert in the world, gets about eight inches of precipitation each year. But deserts in Antarctica get less than two inches a year!

The cold deserts are the hardest places for plants and animals to live. But even here, God has created strange and wonderful creatures and plants. Foxes, small birds, and insects live in cold deserts. Where there are few plants, there are few animals. This is because small animals eat plants, and bigger animals eat small animals. No plants means no animals. In Antarctic deserts, called the "Dry Valleys," the largest animals are microscopic worms that eat bacteria.

Cold desert regions are delicate. It takes many years, sometimes hundreds, to grow plants in the thin soil. The plants that do grow there must be able to hold on to life during the dry time, which is most of the time. In many cold deserts, the only plant life that can be found is moss or *lichen* clinging to rocks.

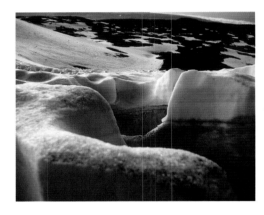

Top **The dry valleys of Antarctica are some of the most severe deserts in the world.**
Bottom **Some deserts have ice, but almost no running water. This is a desert on top of a Hawaiian volcano called Mauna Kea.**

Right **This brilliant white glacier stands in sharp contrast to the rugged mountains behind the glacial plain.**

DESERTS OF THE BIBLE

He will dwell in the parched places of the desert, in a salt land where no one lives.

Jeremiah 17:6

Above **Qumran is a place in the wilderness of Judah where ancient copies of books from the Bible were found.**

The earliest leaders of God's people, Abraham, Isaac, Jacob, and Joseph, lived in a fingernail-shaped green land between mountains and deserts. This place of palm trees and reeds was watered by three rivers, the Euphrates, the Tigris, and the Nile. It was called Mesopotamia. At the edge of the Arabian Desert, Abraham grew up among the mud brick houses in Ur, one of the world's first cities. Mesopotamia was also the home of the Babylonians and the Assyrians, who built wondrous cities and kept the Hebrews in captivity.

At the other end of this green land were the deserts of the Sahara in Africa, Nubia, and Sinai. In the middle of these deserts was Egypt. Egyptians built magnificent stone pyramids and temples. Moses was a great man of Egypt, but he later found out he was really a Hebrew. He became the leader of the Hebrews, and took them across the Red Sea. The Hebrews wandered in the Negev and Sinai deserts for forty years.

Desert people lead nomadic lives. That means that they travel from place to place, looking for water and food for their herds. They usually live in tents, kind of like camping all the time. Many Bible people lived this way. Often, they traveled on God's desert car, the camel. Camels do not have water in their humps, but they do have fat, and this fat helps them keep cool. The camel's body can turn its fat into water, so the camel can go without drinking for a long time. To a camel, a sixty-pound hump is like eight gallons of water!

Left **The Egyptians were one of many peoples who made their home in the desert. They built houses, temples, and palaces.**

DESERTS IN GOD'S PLAN

In a desert land he found him…He shielded him and cared for him; he guarded him as the apple of his eye.
                                                                    Deuteronomy 32:10

God has used the desert as a place to help people get ready to do important things. Before they were ready to go to the Promised Land of Canaan, the Hebrews spent forty years in the Negev and Sinai deserts. In Hebrew, *Negev* means "dry," and it is a very dry place.

Moses went into the Midian desert to be a shepherd for forty years before he became the leader of Israel. The prophet Elijah went into the desert, where God spoke to him and sent ravens to feed him.

Above **The deserts of Palestine help people to get ready for God's important missions.**

Usually, when the Bible talks about the wilderness, it is talking about desert regions. The Judean wilderness was also a desert, and it was very important in God's plan. David hid from Saul there, until he was ready to be the new king of Israel. John the Baptist preached in the Judean desert, and it was there that the Good Samaritan of Jesus' parable took care of the man beaten by robbers.

Perhaps most important of all, Jesus went into the Judean desert for forty days before He started His ministry. He was tempted by Satan, and He used the word of God to fight Satan's attacks. But God wasn't finished using deserts. Many scholars feel that the apostle Paul spent three years after his conversion in an Arabian desert preparing for what Jesus called him to do. Paul became one of the greatest missionaries of all time, sharing the good news that Jesus is alive, and that God can make our lives rich and full.

Right **Moses on Mount Sinai.**
Right Inset **This ancient fortress is in the Judean wilderness.**

FORESTS AND JUNGLES AROUND THE WORLD

Let the fields be jubilant, and everything in them. Then all the trees of the forest will sing for joy. Psalm 96:12

One quarter of all the Earth's land is covered by forests. Forests are beautiful places with trees, bushes, and many creatures. Forests grow on the sides of mountains, in valleys, and in low plains where it rains a lot.

People use many things from the forests. These green places give us lumber for making homes and buildings, and many medicines come from their plants.

Trees and plants protect soil from being washed away by rain. They also make our air fresh by breathing in gases like carbon dioxide and breathing out fresh oxygen. The first place the Bible talks about, the Garden of Eden, was probably a forest.

God has put three kinds of forests on Earth: tropical rain forests (often called *jungles*), temperate hardwood, and *boreal* or *conifer* forests. Tropical rain forests have the richest life. There may be one hundred different kinds of trees in just one square mile.

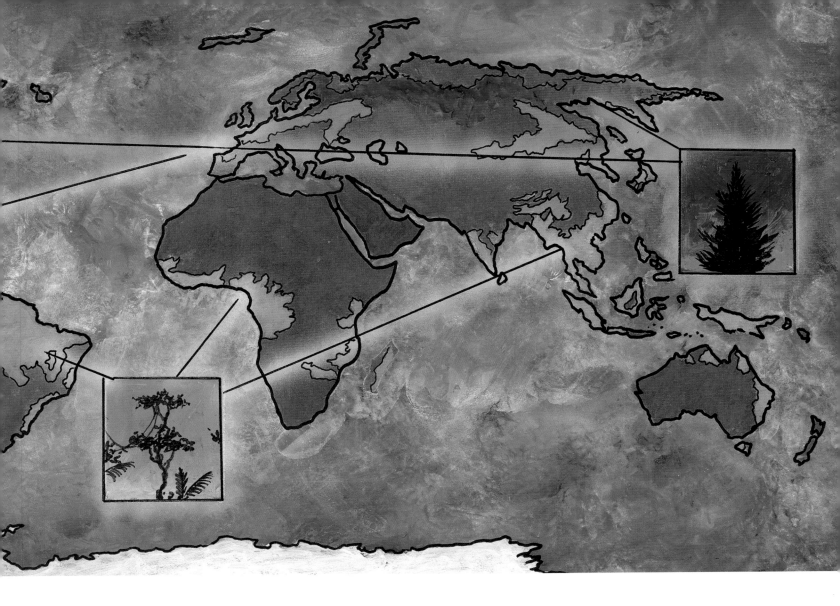

Boreal and temperate areas are found in drier or colder places, and have only a few different kinds of trees.

Forests have more life than deserts. If you could pile up all the plants in an acre of desert land, the plants would weigh anywhere between 270 and 2,500 pounds. But in a temperate forest an acre holds about 80,000 pounds of plants and trees! Most of God's land plants and creatures live in forests.

Above **This world map shows us the three types of forests and their locations.**
Left **Forests can be very dense.**

THE JUNGLES

And rain fell on the earth forty days and forty nights. Genesis 7:12

If you live in a tropical rain forest, there is one thing you will say almost every day: "Hey, it's raining!" It takes a lot of rain and hot days to make a tropical rain forest grow. It rains for many months during the *monsoon* part of each year. Many rain forests are dense and tangled, and we call them jungles. Jungles grow in South and Central America, Central Africa, Southeast Asia, and parts of Australia. One fourth of all medicines at your drugstore came from tropical rain forests. Jungle plants give us pineapples, peanuts, bananas, lemons, eggplants, and even rubber.

Top **Iguassu Falls is deep in the rain forest of Brazil.**

Half of Earth's creatures call the rain forest home, and many live in the trees. The tall trees there have hundreds of different animals, insects, and even little plants growing on them. Many animals spend their entire lives living in the trees, eating nuts and fruits that grow at the very top (called the *canopy*).

Other things live on the forest floor, where it is wet. Some plants live on dead leaves and bark that fall from the trees. They are called *saprophytes,* and include strange mushrooms and beautiful orchids. But it is so dark on the floor of the jungle that not many plants can grow. The action is up in the trees.

Another kind of rain forest is the temperate rain forest. These jungles grow where it is cooler than in the tropics, but where it still rains a lot. The Olympic National Forest in Washington State is one of these. It is the only rain forest in North America.

Left **Many different kinds of life are found at the different levels of the jungle, from the floor to the canopy. This painting shows creatures from jungles all over the world. See if you can find the tiger, stilt house, emerald tree boa, toucan, Giant Rafflesia Flower, poison toad, bat, flying lizard, pangolin, and howler monkey.**
Left Inset **Brightly colored birds live in the rain forests of South and Central America.**

The Temperate Hardwood Forests

I have cut down its tallest cedars, the choicest of its pines. I have reached its remotest parts, the finest of its forests. 2 Kings 19:23

Above **Redwood trees have some of the hardest wood of any tree.**

Trees in temperate forests grow farther apart than the ones in rain forests. Lots of sunlight reaches the ground, so more plants can grow. Some trees like the Scotch pine have needles instead of leaves. Other trees that drop their leaves in fall, sleep during the winter, then grow leaves again in the spring are called *deciduous* trees. The beautiful change in the seasons can best be seen in deciduous forests, where the springtime blooms with lots of bright flowers and buds, the summer has full green leafed trees, and the fall brings yellow, orange, and red to the leaves before they fall for the winter. Someone has said that in the fall, God becomes the artist of the forests, painting them bright colors.

A deciduous forest begins as a meadow with grasses and weeds. When these plants get tall enough, there is enough shade on the ground for woody plants and baby trees, called *saplings*, to grow. The saplings grow up into huge trees, and bingo—you have a forest. A forest like this takes about twenty-five years to grow! It is home to many animals, including rabbits, raccoons, deer, bears, and mountain lions.

Trees are one of God's best gifts to us. When trees are cut into lumber, they can be used to create buildings, bridges, and ships. They can also be used for small things like furniture and toys. People grind up wood to make paper, and many people across the world use wood to heat their homes and cook food.

Right **Fall colors in Zion National Park.**
Right Inset **These temperate forest trees in Yosemite National Park are deciduous, and will drop their leaves when winter comes.**

THE BOREAL FORESTS

For every animal of the forest is mine, and the cattle on a thousand hills. Psalm 50:10

Top **Boreal forests grow in high mountains or where it is cold.**
Bottom **Neuschwanstein castle is nestled in a forest in Germany.**

Boreal forests, or *taiga*, grow in a band across the top of the world where winters are cold and dry, and summers bring melting ice and soggy ground. Most trees in boreal forests are conifer trees, or trees with thin needle-shaped leaves and pinecones. The taiga doesn't have as many different kinds of trees and animals as other forests. Some forests have only one kind of tree for hundreds of square miles. Boreal forests look like gigantic Christmas tree lots, with spruces, firs, and pine trees.

It's COLD in the taiga, and just lasting through the winter is hard. Most conifer trees keep their needles all year long. Unlike a deciduous leaf, each needle is coated with wax to keep the tree from losing water when it gets cold. The needles also have natural antifreeze, just like a car has, to keep them from freezing. God thought of antifreeze long before people did!

Coniferous trees also have long roots that stay near the surface of the ground to get any water as soon as the snow melts. The needles keep the tree warm, and the shape of the trees helps the snow to slide off. Conifers are the tallest living things on earth. Some Redwood trees grow taller than a 36-story building! One giant Sequoia in California weighs more than 2,100 tons, heavier than fourteen blue whales!

You won't find any whales in the taiga, but you will find reindeer, bears, foxes, and other wildlife.

Right **A moose is wading in a marsh. Snow is falling, but we can see strands of evergreen against the snowy mountains.**

APPRECIATING GOD'S DESIGN

The desert and the parched land will be glad; the wilderness will rejoice and blossom. Isaiah 35:1

God's world has wet places and dry ones, and in each He has placed special plants, animals, and people. The world is made to be in balance, with just the right amount of deserts, jungles, oceans, mountains, and valleys. But in many places, people are changing this balance.

Above **Farmers have cut away the tropical forest here to grow food.**

As more and more people use wood, our forests are shrinking. Farmers sometimes cut down or burn forests to clear the land to raise crops for food, and ranchers cut down trees to make pastures for cattle and sheep. Every eight minutes, an entire square mile of tropical rain forest is being cut down! When the forest is destroyed, so are the homes of many animals. Forests help to hold soil together in rainstorms. When rains come and there are no trees, the soil is washed away and nothing can grow. This is called *erosion*. If there is enough erosion, what was once forest turns into desert. We have seen that deserts are beautiful, but so are forests. There must be room for both.

In many places, governments have passed laws to stop the cutting down of trees, and many people are replanting trees in places where logging or farming have destroyed the forest. But it takes many years for a forest to grow back. God calls us to take care of the forests and deserts. Both are special to Him, and make His world the beautiful place it is.

Left **A bright green sapling sprouts against the grey backdrop of a forest that has burned.**

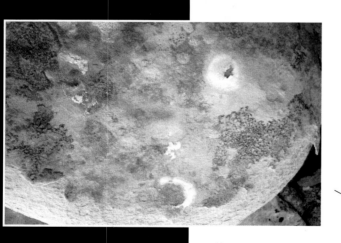

Glossary

boreal (BOR-ee-al) **forest:** a forest that grows where it is cold.

canopy (CAN-e-pee): the tops of the trees in a jungle, where many things live.

conifer (CON-i-fer): a tree with cones and needle-like leaves.

deciduous (de-SIJ-oo-us) **tree:** a tree that drops its leaves in the autumn and grows new ones each spring.

dust devil: a small windstorm like a miniature tornado.

erosion (ee-ROW-zhun): when soil is washed away by wind or water.

jungle: a dense forest rich with life.

lichen (LIE-ken): a tiny scale-like plant that grows on rocks.

mesas (MA-suzs): flat rocky cliffs sticking out of piles of sand; usually found in desert regions.

monsoon (mahn-SOON): The part of each year in tropical areas where it rains for many months.

oasis (o-A-sis): a wet place in the desert, usually fed by an underground spring.